W9-ATY-943

# How to use this book

This book is divided into three parts. The cover and centre colour pages form the castle. The black and white pages of figures, weapons and other things are for you to pull out, colour in and cut out. The other colour pages, including this one, are full of history about castles and information about the people who lived in them as well as fun activities. Don't pull these pages out. There is a glossary on the inside back cover to help you understand special castle words.

Open the cover into a triangle. Fold the smaller flap over the book and push the castle tabs into the slots. Place on a flat surface.

Attach the three walls to the castle. Let battle commence!

Bend the walls over to the side and close the book for storage.

Colour the pictures before cutting them out.

Keep all the cutouts in an envelope and tuck this into the book.

## Templates

Tape a piece of tracing paper over the template or image. Trace in pencil.

Turn the tracing paper over and scribble over the lines with a pencil.

Turn over again and tape on to card or paper. Re-trace firmly over the lines.

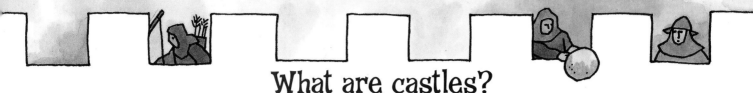

# What are castles?

Castles were large fortified buildings. They were the homes of kings and powerful lords or nobles. Most were built in the Middle Ages (AD 1000–1500). Nobles in Europe and the Middle East defended their land with castles. William the Conqueror built lots of castles in England and Wales. He also built the Tower of London.

The first castles were made of wood. They were built on mounds of earth and surrounded by ditches. They were called MOTTE and BAILEY castles. Later castles were built of stone.

TOWER OF LONDON, ENGLAND

ANGERS CASTLE, FRANCE
Built by King St Louis in the 13th century, this castle had 17 towers and a moat.

ALCAZAR, SPAIN
This huge castle was built by Christians after they took the city of Segovia from the Muslim Moors in the 11th century.

KRAK des CHEVALIERS, SYRIA
This CONCENTRIC castle was first a Muslim fortress but was taken over and rebuilt by the Knights Hospitaller (French crusaders) in the 12th century.

TURKU CASTLE, FINLAND
Finland's oldest medieval castle was built in the 13th century by invading Swedes.

Castles were built to protect the local people. They had thick walls and small slits for windows. They were built on hills, rock and cliff edges. They had MOATS, ditches and walls around them. This made it difficult for an enemy to attack.

It was always difficult to get through the castle gate. It had a PORTCULLIS and DRAWBRIDGE (if it had a moat).

They were very expensive to build and took a very long time to finish. Harlech Castle in Wales was started in 1283 and took seven and a half years to build. At one stage 1,000 men from all over Britain were working on it .

# Castle life

A castle was a little world of its own.

Inside the walls were stables and gardens with fruit and herbs, for cooking and medicines.

There were kennels, a blacksmith, a bakery, a chapel and even a jail.

Servants made and mended armour. Carpenters and stone masons mended the castle.

Bee hives gave wax and honey.

There were fishponds and a well. This was very important for clean drinking water.

Flour, vegetables and meat came from farmers in the countryside.

The Great Hall was the biggest room in the castle. While everyone ate, jesters made them laugh.

Fires burned all year round in the kitchen, cooking the food.

Toilets were built into the castle's outer walls and emptied into a moat or pit.

Castles were not nice to live in. They were cold, damp and dark. There was no glass in the windows. They had log fires for cooking and keeping warm.

Light came from candles and torches made of twigs and straw.

There was very little furniture. They kept everything in wooden chests.

They hung sewn pictures on the walls, called tapestries. These helped to warm the rooms.

Tapestries often showed countryside and hunting scenes.

What pictures would you choose to cover your walls? A seaside scene? A city? Your friends?

# Attack and defence

If a castle didn't give in to an enemy attack, the enemy had to try something different.

They could surround the castle to stop anyone going in or out. Then the people inside starved to death unless they gave in. This was called a SIEGE.

They could tunnel under the walls. They could break down the castle gates with BATTERING RAMS. Or they could use catapults to fire arrows, rocks or dead animals over the walls to kill those inside.

A more dangerous attack was to use a BELFRY to climb the castle walls.

BELFRY
A tower on wheels. Soldiers climbed up inside to try to get over the castle walls.

* Colour the pictures, then cut them out. Cut around dotted line or cut around outline.

SWORDSMEN

LANCE THROWER

ARCHER

SHIELD

SHIELD

ARCHER

LANCE THROWER

SWORDSMEN

* Colour and cut out. Bend the flap under the feet and stand up.

FARMER

HARVESTING PEASANTS

PEASANT FAMILY

LADDER

KNIGHTS FIGHTING

TREBUCHET (GIANT CATAPULT)

* If you would like more
of any of the pictures,
use the instructions
on the first page
and trace them on
to stiff paper.

JOUSTING KNIGHT

HERALD

## GATEHOUSE OF OUTER WALL

### DRAWBRIDGE

* Fold along the line at the bottom of the door and bend the drawbridge over the door. Colour the back of the drawbridge. Take a needle and 40 cm black thread. From the BACK, push the needle through the gate where marked with the spot. (Hold up to the light to see the spot.) WITHOUT pulling the thread right through, push through the spot on the drawbridge, then across to the other spot and through to the second spot on the door. Knot the ends of the thread at the back. Pull on the loop to pull up the drawbridge.

* Glue a toothpick on to the end of the flag and tape it to the castle.

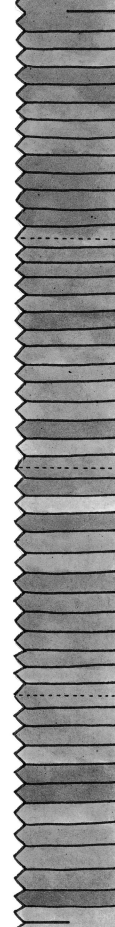

## ENCLOSURE FOR ANIMALS

Fold along dotted lines and cut slots at either end. Slot together to form a square.

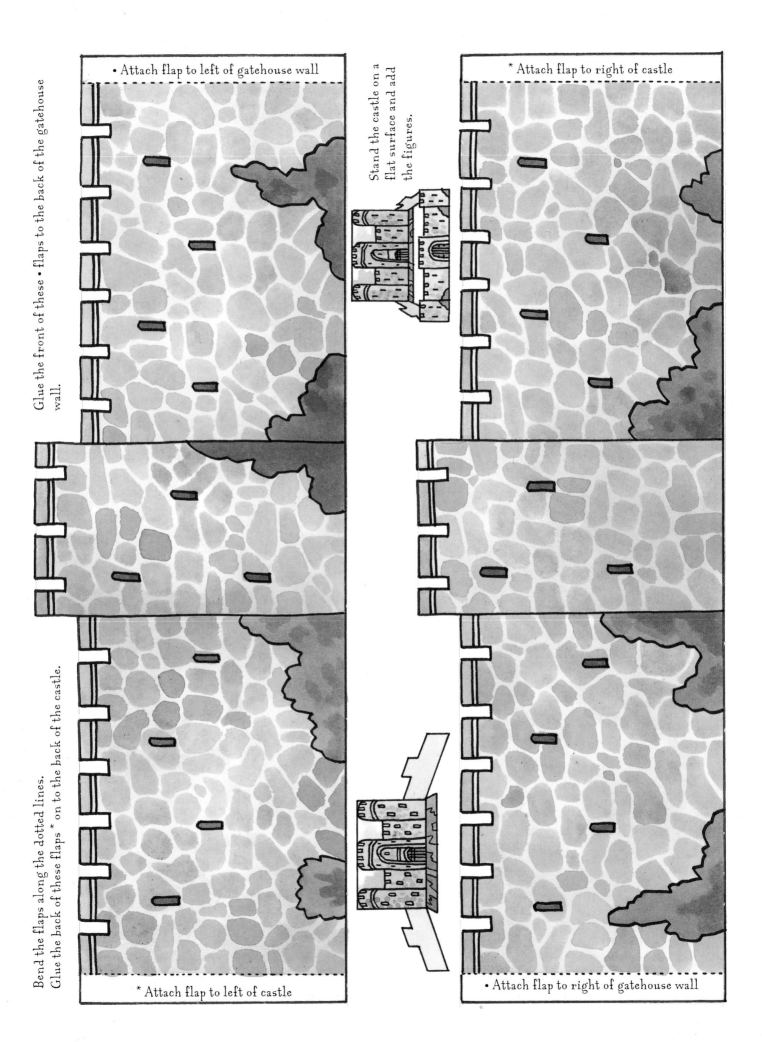

Attach flap to left of gatehouse wall

Glue the front of these • flaps to the back of the gatehouse wall.

Stand the castle on a flat surface and add the figures.

* Attach flap to right of castle

Bend the flaps along the dotted lines.
Glue the back of these flaps * on to the back of the castle.

* Attach flap to left of castle

• Attach flap to right of gatehouse wall

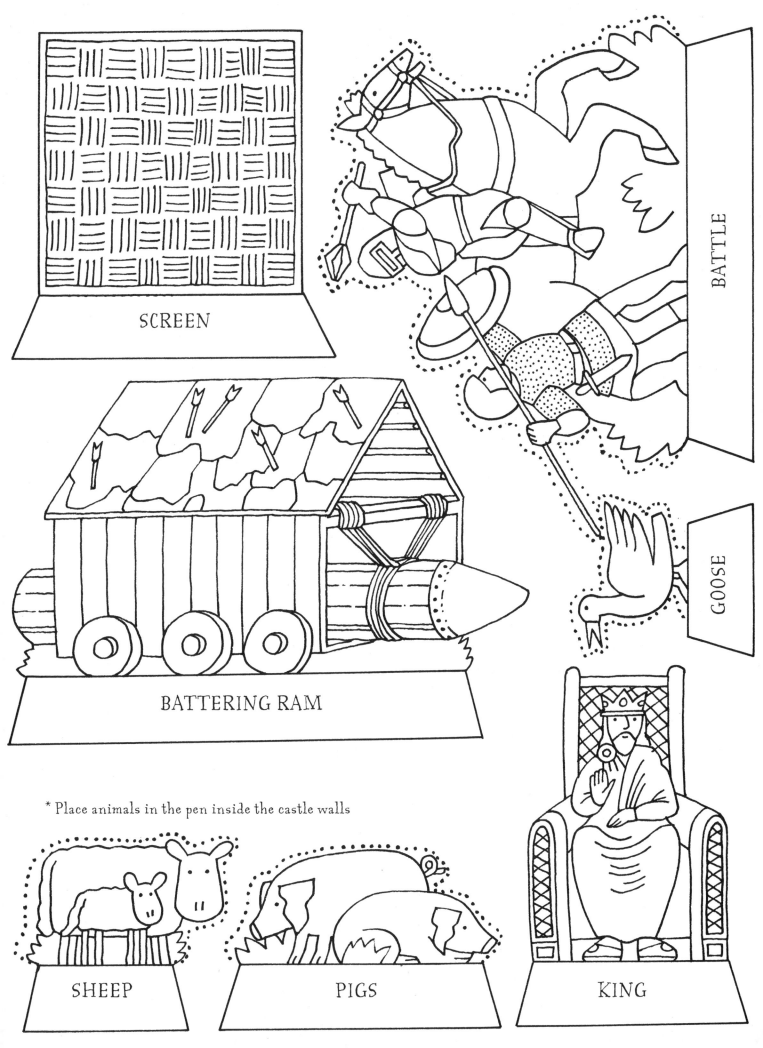

SCREEN

BATTLE

GOOSE

BATTERING RAM

* Place animals in the pen inside the castle walls

SHEEP

PIGS

KING

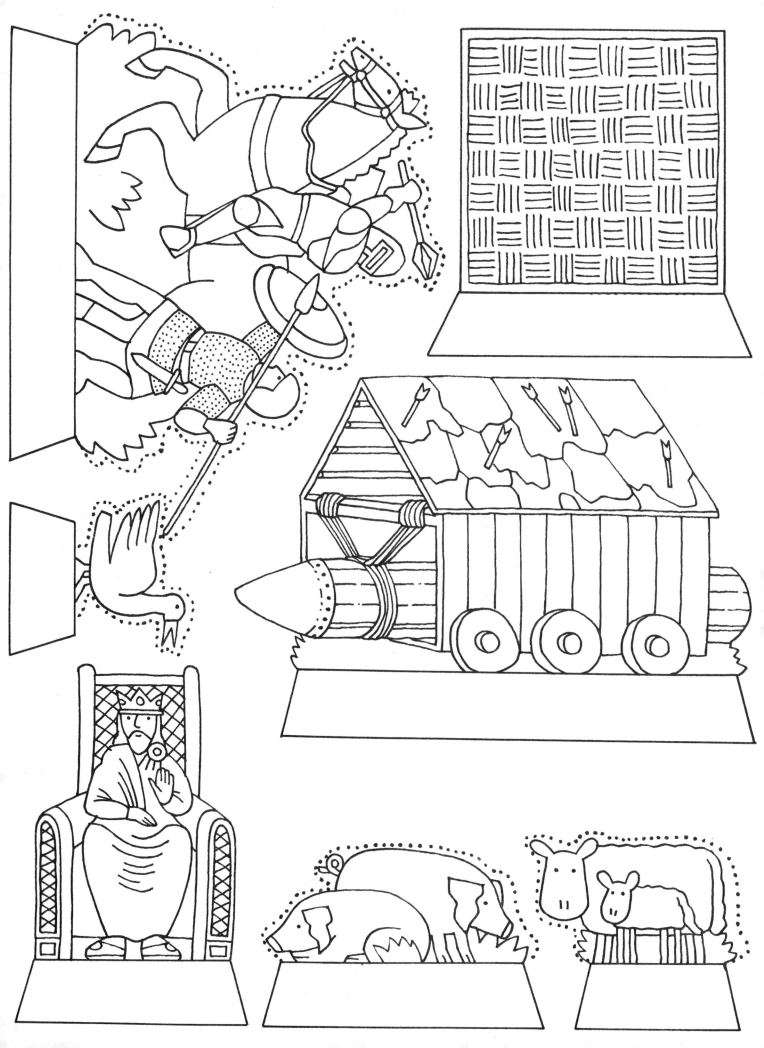

* These tents were very bright and colourful.

LADIES OF COURT

KNIGHT WAITING TO JOUST

* Trace two more jousting knights. Leave off the flaps. Glue card strips or sticks on the back and play jousting games!

STEWARD DRESSING KNIGHT FOR FIGHTING

JOUSTING KNIGHT

The people inside the castle defended themselves with weapons like those used by their attackers, such as bows and arrows. They also poured hot oil and threw down rocks, water and ash. They pushed ladders away with giant boat hooks.

BATTERING RAM
A heavy beam of wood. About twelve men swung this against the gate and walls. It often hung inside a 'penthouse' (shelter) to protect the invaders.

MAT

TREBUCHET
A gigantic catapult for throwing rocks and boulders.

MANTLET
A screen.

BALLISTA
A huge crossbow for firing bolts. It was very accurate and could fire up to 400 metres.

# Knights

The daughters of rich and noble families were brought up to be ladies. They learnt to sew, dance and ride.

The sons were taught to become knights (mounted warriors).

From the age of seven until twenty-one a son learnt everything from riding and fighting to looking after his squire or knight. If he did well, he would be knighted. This was called DUBBING.

Christian knights fighting Holy Wars were called CRUSADERS. When they were not fighting in wars, knights looked after their land and castles and served their king.

# Tournaments

Tournaments were splendid, colourful battle games.

A JOUST was a fight between two knights on horseback. They charged at each other and tried to knock each other off with their lances.

The weapons were blunted but it was very dangerous and knights were often wounded and even killed.

Knights fought on horseback dressed in armour and used a sword, a lance, an axe, a mace or a flail. They also held a shield.

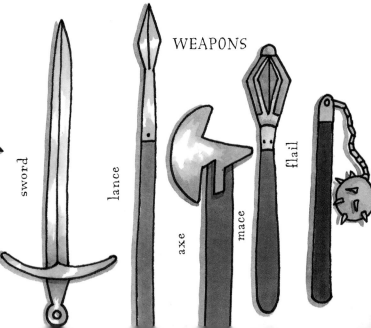

WEAPONS

sword lance axe mace flail

# Chivalry

Chivalry told knights how to behave. A knight must:
✣ honour and protect noble ladies
✣ keep his word
✣ be loyal to his lord and friends
✣ be generous to defeated enemies
But knights did not have to treat ordinary people in this way.

## Armour

The first knights wore shirts made out of CHAIN MAIL to protect the top of their bodies.

Later, armour was made of solid metal plates covering the whole body. The pieces were joined together with rivets and leather straps. Knights also wore helmets.

chain mail

Sometimes horses wore armour too.

This knight is dressed in armour from the year 1210. He's wearing chain mail and a linen tunic (surcoat).

Use the instructions on the first page to trace and cut out this knight.

Put a shield design here. (see inside back cover).

Make a row of knights with different coats of arms.

# Dungeons

Underneath the castle were the dungeons where they kept prisoners.

Some dungeons were called 'oubliettes'. This is a French word that means 'locked away and forgotten'.

Some prisoners were chained to the walls with a heavy iron rings round their necks and legs.

# Heraldry

When knights wore armour which covered them completely, it was impossible to know who they were.

It was very important in battle to see who were your friends and who were your enemies, so knights started to paint their own patterns on their tunics. They became known as 'coats of arms'.

The king ordered his heralds to keep records of these patterns and that is how heraldry began.

The most common shape for a shield is the 'heater' (or flat iron). Women's shields were lozenge-shaped.

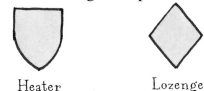

Heater      Lozenge

Coats of arms are still made today.